Zero Summer

by Andrew Demcak

BlazeVOX [books]

Buffalo, New York

for Peter, of course

Acknowledgments

"American Gothic," "Automated Response to Mark Strand," "In the Lives of Men, There's No Golden Paint," "Kept Image," "Myself in Memoirs," "Subject Matter" all appeared in slightly different versions in the on-line literary journal *Elimae*

"American Gothic," "The Newlyweds," "Noah," "Three Against One" all appeared in slightly different versions in *Asspants*

"Before Dawn at Bluff Cove" appeared in *The Wisconsin Review*

"Black Hair, Blue Eyes," "Candidate" both appeared in the online literary journal *Melancholia's Tremendous Dreadlocks*

"Cannulae" appeared in *Juked,* and was also a nominee for *The Pushcart Prize 2007*

"Cyst" appeared in *Skidrow Penthouse*

"Giorgio di Chirico, 1914," "Silk Road" "Unknown Pleasures," appeared in the on-line journal *Seconds*

"God and the 3rd Step" was published in *Eight Octaves Magazine*

"Heroin Days" appeared in the Hasting College, Nebraska's *Plain Songs*

"Interzone," "Perfectionist at the Beach," and "Scarecrow" all were printed by *Pearl*

"Suicide Note for Weldon Kees" appeared in the *Pebble Lake Review*

"Teeth on the Faithful Bit" was published by *Chiron Review* in a slightly different version.

* * *

A pre-publication 20 poem excerpt of *Zero Summer* appeared online on the Belgian website *The Argonaut's Boat* at: http://users.skynet.be/spier/argoboatdemcak.htm

My endless gratitude to:

Kaya Oakes, Didi Menendez, Geoffrey Gatza, Steve Mueske, Grady Harp (my favorite critic), David Spiher & Ralph Thurlow, Brenda Hillman, Bob Hass, Joan Larkin, Richard Siken, Justin Chin, Larry Kaplun, Dorianne Laux and Joe Millar, Randall Mann, Nina Lindsay, John Vick, Tony Trigilio & Shimmy, J. P. Dancing Bear @ *The American Poetry Journal*, Amanda Auchter @ *Pebble Lake Review*, Cooper Renner @ *elimae*, Clay Banes @ Pegasus Books, J. Michael Wahlgren, the OPL gang: Garry Lambrev, Paul Schiesser & Jamie Turbak, Carlon Yoder, Maria Ramirez, Isis Rios, Dale Jones; Katherine Hastings @ Word Temple, Owen Hill @ Moe's Books, James "Ziggy" Winburn @ Citizen Poets, Alex Green @ *Caught in the Carousel*, Johnny @ Boss Robot Hobby, Amy & Mike Antongiovanni, Jamie Deetz, Carla Aiello & David Renshaw, Christopher Münch & Aaron Brown – my film-makers, my AA posse: Rossi, Doug, Hector, Jose, Pat & Bobbie, Jim G., Bill H., David B., John S., Tom, Andrew, and also the SF GuyWriters: Anthony, Jay, Mac, Jim, Richard, Derrick; of course: Carol & Jack Demcak, Tonny & Isolde, Chris & Janice Demcak, George & Larry for always being next door, Camille & Steve, Dave & Ron, James, Nnekay, all of my Facebook pals, Beulah, Bink, Calico, & Outdoor Cat, and all my editors, publishers, and future rejecters. If I forgot your name in this book, not to worry; I have many more books on the way.

Contents:

PART 3
...a bloom more sudden
Than that of summer, neither budding nor fading,

...Between melting and freezing
The soul's sap quivers. There is no earth smell
Or smell of living thing. This is the spring time
But not in time's covenant. Now the hedgerow
Is blanched for an hour with transitory blossom
Of snow, a bloom more sudden
Than that of summer, neither budding nor fading,
Not in the scheme of generation.
Where is the summer, the unimaginable
Zero summer?

T. S. Eliot
from *Four Quartets,*
"Little Gidding"

Zero Summer

PART 1

...Between melting and freezing

Zero Summer

the cotton of dove song spun through birches
chorus of ants
scored andante
on
pale stucco

I'm a skinny piano
waiting
for his hands to compose the air

in the whistling grass next door
the cat
digests a cricket's lonely mandolin

the dog's penis sings its red aria

gnats blink half-notes
mating
over the bars of patio chairs

my skin listening

still no accompanist: I can't kiss me!

and the sperm's tempo
always insisting

Interzone

I lay before him this way:
a channel
newly cut
a leading under

but he
wouldn't touch water unless it meant sex
his dowser
his divining rod
a hand
that could pin things to the bed

because I
flow I am not
because I flow I am
not here

distance was a liquid swimming
between held breaths
between contractions of
words

he presented his cavalcade of
names for me:

Erie
Panama
Suez

Silk Road

I take it up the ass because I want
him to stay
snow-stained
like a silkworm

I'm threaded
eye of the needle
and all
of that-

just as Cavafy wrote:
his street
boys using themselves up
sticky-hipped

I am a porcelain bead to be strung
a skeleton
whose bones are siphoned
and evaporated like milk

but I
want him to stay
this night
or however
long it can be tailored
cocooned

I
must be woven over his condom sleeve
and spun
all the way down the Aegean

Insight
(for Grady Harp)

pages turned
one hand sticky as blue
liver

naked dots
nothing but paper

reading into white
tanlines
his forget-
me-nots or
wheat? or cocoa?

Adonic
long and short of it
suffer for our sex
in high-gloss print

all this hidden beneath
shaving-cream sink
nightbedded
boxed or
closeted

peculiar heat

"disease"
of idle fingers
before afternoon
shower
or because of morning pup-tent

coughing up from the skin purse
a jackpot

Vincent V. in 1993

(For Christopher Münch)

someone
(*you?*)
speaking above a louder
noise
I couldn't understand it
something
terrible I was trying to be told
amputated
your collect call
(from where?
from Hollywood?)
interrupted

how like
us
once I was wired
to your bed-springs
an aluminum ear
then I was cut
off
busy signals around the bedroom
like fatal crows

now the mute landlady
brushing around the trash cans
going
gone
no sounds of the sweeping away
only
disconnected bricks
and the quiet
isolation
of this half-eaten peach

Unknown Pleasures

last-call cruising fueled by screwdrivers
2 a.m. chances
while bar lights blink on

how could I not think of Genet's *Querelle*?
fog-tissued docks
sperm dealt like perfect
opium
50 francs per fly button
pass it on

his penis magnetic

O
lost metal of me!

but where could he be?
cock swaggering
shadowed in pant leg
cum-stained
the navy medals flashing

just an unattainable character
an empty passenger seat
the streetlight
fracturing through water on my lashes

Cannulae
(for J. Michael Wahlgren)

agitated again
adolescent

the ocean
turned
in a gorgeous knot

lymph recited into harbors of love:

urchin beds
the octopus' shell hole

ships interrogating the bay
pounding
at receptive vessels
the passengers of youth

or was it simpler than that:
a teen-age promise
of sex
taken back
beneath the black dripping lips
of the cove?

Venus in Furs
(for Anne Gray Sexton)

his needle in my grease
he thinks I am
the haystack

we play house with our two girls
who are rubber frogs
their mouths painted on

Darling
did you know that the sunshine is
only cardboard?
I dress like A. Sexton
in some advertised clothes?
I drink word-
bringing gin
that correction fluid?

in
the morning I bag his lunch
while we fuck
my spine flat on the ironing board

at
night
inside the moon's Valium
he'll feed
lipstick into my incubator
so my asshole
will match my Italian shoes

Untogether

no longer "you and I"
a car passing
crates of roadside cabbages
thrown dirt from
the heart's burning shovel

I was not your
picnic plate
shucked cob
obedient
pepper
your autumn tree dimpled with
gorgeous apples

you sent me to muddy
purgatory

who needed these months of
old potatoes
their sprouts unbuttoned
at your shoes?

our relationship
that old
moon-life
that dry garden of years ago

Prince Charming

and the ambiguousness of your ease

I've Got You Under My Skin
I must have
sat pondering that phrase later when you
pulled me near

you'd rather we'd fuck than eat

your silk cummerbund
cinders under my
fingernails

what fun when you stiffened
against me with the words like beguiling
and wooed
your tongue's muscular orders

someone placed perfectly for a kiss
a midnight ball
a proven Cole Porter

Dead Man's Cock
(for J T)

it hangs colder than chrome

how I left you
what was unspoken like gasoline fumes
surrounding us
our spark near that danger
your father pounding the door to your bedroom
when I was there
the make-believe boy
that greased your gears

as night unfolded
intricate maps
without directions
my tongue knew the quick route to your zipper

but you kept racing
pedal stiff to the floor
leaning into the blind curve of my spine

what eventually took you from me-
not the ocean and her feathery wash
but a motorcycle
burning pistons
blackened beyond a jump-start

now I
keep you in the concern of an oil cloth
hallowed

that discontinued part

Scarecrow
(for Matthew Shepard, 1976 – 1998)

If our scarecrow back home could do that,
the crows would be scared to pieces.
-Dorothy Gale, Kansas

The biting itch of those posts.

Whose hands were meant for such nagging ants?

Last night,
tequila soured breath,
that man, (or was it two of them,
both young, your age?)

Sweat melting the shyness on your tongue.

Now you ask,
where is that moon of a few moments ago?
a mouth drooling open
how did morning come to fill these lungs?

Your arms rope-and-nail hung,
eyes blood-painted,
chest stuffed with punches.

A danger sign on the split rail fence.

-Proceed At Your Own Risk
Keep To The Right-

Lit upon
by those birds who refused to take flight.

Before Dawn at Bluff Cove

oval of crow swoop jet against the sky

my parents in yards of cream bunting
their
wax bodies knifed like butter
ghosts whom
I denied all my childhood

Our
Lady of Convenience sobbed and drank
while
dinner sat rotting
rock salt and hog fat
in the mortuary

bloody comfort
oxides of forgetting
formaldehyde's
aroma
filling the fenced-in rooms

a shallow plate passed like inheritance

Cheater

You come home all second-hand potatoes

what am I to eat
dressed up for your
undoing?

hadn't you scraped that boyfriend
from your hasty bed
his cock
a peeling
that made me pause?

O the steady crush of
your tongue
always fooling me with sugar

how my complexion curved towards your
cancerous bread
your black grain

run along
now
my bent blade
but leave me your butter

Unpacking

moving truck limping into the wind
mud
guards besmirched
austere words unboxed

you and I pawing at decisions
there-
the dapper shoulders of couched silk
some
grandfather's leather chair
then my ex's
letters
that perennial argument

and I thought about leaving you again

in the gutter a desiccated cat
appalling
nothing but urgent belly
its eyes as immaculate as a doll's

The Newlyweds

so what if you'll drink until 3 a.m.
bullying that side road of Morpheus

O dead category!
your lock-and-ball
fury

this marriage wasn't wide enough

the shot glass windowing a magazine
face
water ring spent
a seminal whim
from *that little war*

diluted relief?

midnight insistent in
the clink of ice
bourbon sweet with
unimagined grief

American Gothic

they followed gravel home
the driveway
to a marriage like a bus disaster

perched in his study
the pulsations
of sperm
their numbered tails fixed to
proffered wire

when she lurched for
the phone call
to practice her mouth
Hello
all lipstick

they chose to eat with the boys
fifteen minutes in the kitchen

good pop
good wife

and fuss about Aunt Dot waving
her lank arms
from some anonymous life

Three Against One

my father nursing each Navy hair on
his knuckles
I held tightly my quiet
brother
while my sister
the prickly pear
sat upwards to read her punished cheek

in the story where the fisherman became
the king
father
spoon-fed as we were
admonishing us to
Eat! God damn it!

he loitered home
 "some quality time
with the children"

drunken
hook-eyed

on his lips the water of a sour sea

Kept Image

a childhood returned
this morning
mother dragging us
needy and feral-
haired

it's my older cousin on top
draining inside of me
yesterday's
first man
desire like pumping water

nights he sailed into me

enlisted
I was 10
pain along the shoals

but how
could I fend off
familiar skin

with what:
my almost fists
my obedient holes?

Other Pursuits
(for P G)

I stood like a dress form in the hall
while you secured every argument

costumed
the pattern of your leaving
its sidelong veneer of blame

I writhed
solemnly
on the velvet pin cushion

I couldn't explain the fraying of seams
fallen hems
the suit of our history-
something
a little bit like Medea's?

didn't I button
and unbutton you
and collect
every mysterious thread?

I suppose now
that it's unimportant
the tailor has gone thimble-blind
too soon
his angry stitches
sewn across the moon

PART 2

…this is the spring time,
But not in time's covenant.

American Poetry

should one live off such slender means
verses
that one could not eat?

patriotic as
baked beans
however tasting of each
other's signatures
or disguised by
coattails and hungry sleeves

that stevedore
unloading his American letters
when braving
bohemian microphones

culled and booked
poets too
from all-electric kitchens
awaiting one tiny
drop
of some patron's pitcher
laboring
over
the soup-bones of literature

Poet

exiled beyond the word's sovereignty
your sentence
its gallery of turned
soil
wanting to be the torment of
the bedroom
or a plastic school jacket

you sought the blue snow-light of antique glass
in midwinter on paper

O tender
yearling

the pale purples
and pure soundless
black
underneath
the thesaurus of earth

those lines
indiscriminate
as truffles
your solitary pig roaming at night

Subject Matter

still your one hand floundering
trying to
write your story with the tide

you wouldn't
return to an empty page when waters
ignited to a color of regret

the teary shallows whispering

sunset
is nothing-
the sea is done

surf crashing
under a tired frigate
busily
rolling
like a woman into a dress
on a bed where you once were welcomed

Best Seller

a circumstance of cypress
and single
spaced lines
pendant
the unread heaven
of text

the analogy of quiet
ruins
scattered like those ordinary
immortals
or so resembling their
chin bones

the living book was exposed
beyond latticed fingers
gathering
of a recurrent font
the lost story

the demon who had sworn not to be caught

Apple in the Dark
(For Clarice Lispector)

realism uprooted

onion stalks
unfurling sweet clean pages

thornier
bougainvillea
wild tiny blooms in
red ropes above Brazilian magnolia

god as writer: frangipani branches
reprinted in
an apple's golden bough

even in this translation:

heat-cracked nouns of
odd stonework
black clotted soil
holy water eroding carnal pods

Automated Response to Mark Strand

what matters is: the bird is in the tree

the eyes
of the reader are
hard and cold

where the fish leaps
from the page
the farmer
in his costume begins to aspire
he will not
have tenderness
to learn from

the fact of the world is
that it is hard
and cold

the poem is a permission
given away

the bird is in the tree
once more
and our hidden self revealed

Blue Eyes, Black Hair

43

we pass
we being our limited *while*
in these arguments
or *during* someone's
jumping

does that lone zero negate our
future
or endow it with a ticking?

let the integers fuss in the bedroom

we are located in an expanse of
now
space stretches its sundial's shadow

so here we are full-bellied
and there
then
emptied

our next moment shaped
with an arc of years
and numbered places

merci à Marguerite Duras

Myself in Memoirs

I'm this close
knee to chest
perceptible
visited by angry philosophers

such news embarrasses me
when training
lions

or American lap dogs

or
those boys awed by the rancor of
slept-in beds

however true to my journal:

Eros
then a few sticky peach peelings
and moonlight
on a dreamed-of ceiling

Eudemonia

we kissed after *Lifting Belly*
Gertrude's
poem shared upstairs
just mentioned

your browsing hand reading my thighs open

tongues coupled
making our jockstraps drop

on the felt couch
we hardened
Aristotles
in concrete

the seminal sparks downstairs

months practicing "Steinese"
among these chairs

In the Lives of Men, There's No Golden Paint

twice a week
the midnight expressionist
scrubbed his oils
perhaps a sleepless
Mondrian
self-conscious as thinning rope

wet forays meditated in
patter
chromatic juxtapositions gave him
no custardy hint
of relationships

things modulated
with respect to some
practical girl

his still-lifes meant nothing:

bottles
flea markets
a few bars of soap

The Greater Than Which Is Nothing

to sleep breathing it all in
a glimmer
through the window
nothingness striated

the trite granulations of stars seen
through a bedside water glass
the braiding
and unbraiding of exiled lights

to stare
emaciated
and worry the stripes
of a half-opened sock drawer

what
to do beached awake
in bunks
under
these nut-colored sheets
with midnight above

insomnia and eyelids that won't shut?

Giorgio di Chirico, 1919

January composed of filmy
structures:

curtains smothered down to sleep

eyes masturbating in extinguished
rooms

the amber lamps of bones

those women
floating by an ossified building
violet shadows of their hair
slipping
out to sea
their acrimonious hips

the pink dusk
siphoned across a sill

unwashed
pale legs laid open

midnight
congealed like carbon

the wind's tongue up
the river's practiced spine
lulled by
an encouragingly oiled shoreline

Saturday in the Park with Duke

all evening like a young man
gone barefoot
spontaneous summer
of a public concert

rhythms persistent
thawing out that indigo devil
and one fragrant strip
of a woman

Mr. Ellington
expatiating

even the catbirds noticed

arithmetic of downbeat
shimmying
into the piano grass
while venerable souls
stood listening

Suicide Note for Weldon Kees

slim thicket
of abandoned chapbooks

my words will recollect
rake-gathered
measured for the heights of crowns
or hooks

eyes grown accustomed to city lights

my jaundiced flame
inexplicable

somehow
oxygen was enough for me

a gasp
an accent: I wasn't local

on the Golden Gate Bridge
car left behind
feet stepping in air
my sun-seeking vines

Drinking

the wind's glove fingered the evening house

you clawed back that regrettable thirst
but drank
after an existential rain

the arbitrariness of gin bottles
rolling down the red staircase of your throat

night had been swallowed
gallons ago
the full cups from the cold-water suburbs
treatments
for the black plumbing of nerves

your
life decanted into a shallow glass
in a beaten town
at sunset
while god
waited for you
like drain in the street

Liberty

that alcoholic in his critical
seat believed god
and the newspaper

hadn't He snapped His fingers just once?

considering the Fall
that person slack
in the office doorway
as nervous as
a thread's unbraiding

he remembered
those lilacs tossed by the evening air
and a chain
pulled to unlink itself
something blurred
like the spots of a leaping
cat

something that had made its quick exit

Petrified

tonight
how neatly it walls me
its stiff
walks and rip-rap
the chafing knuckles of
granite
and that narcotic moon glinting
plastered into flint-colored oaks

on the slate of this pastoral rehab
I swallow Valium like gravel
each
pill in its scheduled place
perfect
an unlit mosaic
deep as a mine
quarried
a cure for this old sickness

while between the pebbled garden paths
two concrete sparrows sit
petrified
their stone beaks sipping an empty bird bath

Heroin Days

the charmed tangle of us

our photo
selling the contusions of haute couture
posed
heroin-chic

that attractive
abscess

the gentle syringe pushed us
to emerge
it lauded something useful
a labyrinth of nerves
its own entrails
unbraiding

our images
set in numbing syrup
the consummate fix
existing
beneath our thumbs
elegant as Prada

Teeth on the Faithful Bit

Burnt money
for the favors of heaven.

You suffer
in an addict's sober hell,
forgetting
the black crayon
of a friend's pleading eye.

You refuse talk of rehab.

Under the labyrinths
of your thin veins,
Jerusalem
wet between your fetlocks.

Kissing you like a Muslim,
lips on lips,
your dealer sold you
the smack crucifix,
his horse-Christ,
a winner's blood in him.

God and the 3rd Step

at first
He was an irrelevant word

then
an unflawed blackberry arriving
in the sun

rosettes of icing along
the valium skyline

the murdered
and living brightness

moon
like my mother
drawn before me

the lesson of the last
vodka
on a high rooftop
a city
where this ache wouldn't end

an airport where
clouds and planes came

some back-lit restaurant

the surprise witness
at my own trial

this distance closing
thin as a needle

PART 3

...a bloom more sudden
Than that of summer, neither budding nor fading,

Airline Disaster on the 11 O'clock News

photograph of one mother's son
a lost
medallion
the backdrop of ocean green

updates
and anchored assurances
shots of victims
or recent bodies

then
back to repeating undercurrents of
words
and the station break to sell toilet
cleaner

angled particularly
a garbed widow
or husband

zoom-in
children fingering a New York shoreline

a parade towards the black Atlantic

Jabberwocky
(for John Wayne Gacy)

bottom floor
in a borrowed clown suit
your hand feeling its way along the rail
to the basement
red rubbing between legs

it's the first sex
the playroom just out of
sight
or sitting in your patient lap
like
polishing a fifth grade trophy
up down

wonderland
that real life experience

every child was perfectly easy
when you performed
a sky coarse
cloudy

Candidate

politics in the apartment corner
my Siamese cat pukes
a grass veto
the primary greased
a contusion

they're sweet on it here: in stomach muscle
in lengths of blood-soft intestine
in knots
of colons
the diplomatic worm mouths'
forced movements
wriggling candidates
that Janus grin promising itself
like a ball of white string
he says
he says

not dead
no de-worming pill
they're writhing
in cat-boxed shit for weeks
the twisting
of a politician's tongue
on TV

Pathetic Fallacy

the Muslim girl
with shawl
Allah's daughter
reading arcane symbols
to her cell phone
lulled by the protection of a black
Hermès head-scarf

I can feel the teenage
nausea flexing in her
like a moth
the miniscule line
that delineates
the interweaving hand of god
punching
out
so that one of us would be able
to touch
the scrim of divine countenance
separating us
during this seven
minute elevator ride

I picture
her ignoring
that cool Christian prix-fixe

how she must taste the ridiculousness
of its seekers
the ones who would choke on
her faith
hungry for His body
His blood

Desert Storm

Saddam Hussein standing in the newscast

intermission
your son's room empty
you
thought your way along a blank wall

didn't
you recognize the unused birthday
candles
that wreath of daffodils
your own
voice
was it still a mother's?

it happened-
he died bone naked
and branded
a hemp
rug blinding his face

difficult as roots
the questions riddling your own two hands

Blindness

the Kurdish boy squints
reading by flashlight
restless
on a red rooftop in Baghdad

downtown
the mosque's blind window opens
upon the widow still crying "He's dead"

that shop-keeper shakes
on evening errands
he applauds
with topsy-turvy passion
an invisible radio somewhere
and salutes a uniform
that runs down
a midnight pair of American legs

this soldier patrolling
a monsoon cloud
eyeless
the regrets of combat boots
his search light
drifts down
an obedient moon

First

in an instant of death
we registered
the shudder of music
a delicate
rehearsal of the spirit world

caskets
arranged
like one of Schoenberg's tone rows

after lunch
in passing
we were served
a score
like a metronome
those pages
of the strange syncopations of space

Saint
Mark's floated away
the mourners in self-deafness
powered by a history
which noted
that one of us
was missing

The Death of Allen Ginsberg

gurus gossiping
ashes
caretakers
white haired and almost rich
hungry ghosts
and one-eyed subway trains of Manhattan
sisters
and smooth invulnerable boys
from Wichita
unsurprised by sex
visiting
this departed one

kindred
his pure belly
St. Patrick's swami
Hare Rama
his urn
their phantom lover

one half elbow
and one half Nirvana

Perfectionist at the Beach

fifteen degrees higher than your elbow
the sun was a Roman coin
as marrow
rinsed from your flesh
its bronze announcing
a high tide
tracing the grayness
of your thigh

alchemical
a fluency
of vein

your suicide
that umbrella
whose plume wouldn't shade a happier shore

an undoubtable need
persistently
penciled by your burden
poetic
a longing for the wordless in your words

Quitting
(for Kaya Oakes and Peter Godeschalk)

twin virgins dying by the birthright
of fire
a mythology was neatly
breathed in

your head was a poor filter
like a bird occasioned with rain
you couldn't shake off
your telling lungs

hadn't
Socrates taken hemlock?

your smokeless
body like a splitting stone
torment
in your lip corner
blood clowning your sputum

death was different
another family

Cyst

a woman caught convincing herself
by way of smoking
this surgery
this red problem
massed in a toiling skin

intimate need of an x-rayed life
overestimating treatments
risk levels
in the early morning light

what
good was remembering one casino-
or toasting that perilous moment
in immortal Italy
at 5:15
breast cancer between the cypress trees?

S. I. D. S.

the flowers of your white concern
days at a time
made up of his warm bottles
and cries
the moonlight echoing
between
hygienic trees

out of the milky crib
his hands
bloomed
up and wondering
this evening

how they worked against
the snow's blue edge
their knowledge
their undercurrents
of light
sallow from months of *wake and feed*

peculiar daffodils
out of season
roots and leaves
whispering towards winter

Coda
(for P W A)

a rhythm revealing itself
under
your tenuous ribs

to die a Bach fugue
enough counterpoint
to finger out of

in the hospice
with lovers untuned
death quietly performing your T-cells

you suffered sweat
that cold metronome

in time
your varnished bones
plus three bars
of silence
would be
the well rehearsed melody
set against
the virus-whine

Migraine

you wished for birch wood
that cold logic
icy leaves in an arc of emptiness

the body was the blood's practiced sleeve

it never took too long for the pain
to arrive
sinking in
hot wine in the head
feeding the ache
an un-stoppered drain

that vicious winter
a huddling
of knives

you listened in yourself for frost
or freezing
your thinking lost in the gaps
then snowy knots
clustered trees
then sleep

Noah

was there still time in the ocean?

half of Eden expected you
reciting page numbers
from the zoo's new inventory

you came with plastic fins
for land animals

your soliloquies
were whatever made you set sail
and retain
your substantial mettle

affairs pounded out
like wooden stalls

in the dripping forest
of hedgehog and zygote
a growl wafted

while worldwide
indignant fools opened umbrellas
and stood
to weep each earthly alphabet

Future Tense

you are the standard prototype
glibly electric
who eked out a living

history remembered
religion believed

what troubled enough
to wish
on a wandering star?

you couldn't imagine another existence

this country's impressive standards
its plastic familiarities

Utopia:
angels arriving daily with iPhones

The New Tenant

you had seen him
under that stale lamplight
and you prayed
for the arch of his spine

O divine architect!
O quick-drying cement!

your thoughts ran down a blind staircase
re-arranging
your lachrymose floor plan
imagining
his un-upholstered divan

but your humble designs
would have to be patient
to halt
at your threshold
commitment straining
your red bricks

he'd be
an unveiling ceremony
you know
every inch of his room
naked below

Offstage

we were a serpent
its tail in its teeth
in love
after the third act
refusing bouquets
the circularity of our scenes
we poor players
of an earlier age

the stage doors were care-worn and cracked

your golden tongue
never lifted itself exactly
earthquakes coiled
in my script

our Eden
surely
waiting offstage

wasn't it always
in the next night's town
its yellow floodlight
or spotlight
shining?

-for Bette D. and Liz T.
and all of their men

Chinese Cinema
(for Le Sheng Liu)

Mandarin stars were still untouchable
defiant
the quick wings of wild geese

the celluloid
of their affordable bodies
in the stiff pews
of a Hong Kong theater

the moon unbound
spilled into darkness
and a plum tree's
unedited grace

Gong Li's comfortable insolence
or shoulder blades
her naked origin
anticipating
the young director's eye
burnished by a bright universe
immediate
that spirit
that little credo-

all possibilities of light

Discoverer of Piltdown Man in Preschool

she pictured that doorway in his skull
the sifting room
his real acquaintance
with shovels

it seemed his mind was twice-sized

sometimes
he stooped in the noon playground
sandcastle readied for scrutiny

she watched his naked intent
digging down-
why?
by some commandment
conceiving
that unmapped street of Babylon
or
the toe ring of a Sumerian priest?

or did he seek some repressed feeling
like a god's molar
inside the psychic earth-
once extracted
his joy was undressed?

Red Cowboy Shirt

childhood
complete with American cotton
and a puzzle of silk brocade

you faded in and out of the closet
in the shaking leaf-printed light

what you felt was earthly-
a boot-shaped feeling

scent of hot rain drifting across the sill
plastic holster
the fluttering curtains
a tin star
all crowded into this room

down to your white t-shirt
like so many Saturdays
then the red cowboy shirt
a ghost
each year expecting
a child's hands
to come buttoning
unbuttoning

Salamander Crossing

(for Brenda Hillman)

in snake-vine tumble of Appalachia
Lingam and Yoni awake

the air is a strain of Copland
a lilting gypsy moth

the fox-run
and far field alike
are no longer fallow

under rot-heavy logs
exclamation points
of red-legged salamanders
punctuate

the females
crossing the males
like suspension bridges
sexual gelatin
her pearly toll
deposited beneath his chin
if scent
complements
she'll complete her goal

she is evergreen:
the forest through a keyhole

Moment of the Yew Tree, Moment of the Rose

wisteria spent itself completely

your twin garlands
over the juice pitchers
the block party pissing its light
into the grass

young peonies
dandelions
frowning white
the summer night
behind ears

no mistaking the tulips
who wanted to kiss you
waiting beneath cautious stars

somewhere
a lover folded like laughter
in dogwood blossom
moonlight
mint and dirt

your heart
as sure-footed as rainwater

Andrew Demcak is the author of the award-winning poetry collection, *Catching Tigers in Red Weather* (2007), which was favorably reviewed by Grady Harp in *Oranges & Sardines*. His writing has been published in print and on-line in many very fine literary journals, popular magazines, and anthologies. His poems, including "Young Man With iPod" (Poetry Midwest, #13), are taught at Ohio State University as part of both its English 110.02 class, "The Genius and the Madman," and in its "American Poetry Since 1945" class. He currently works as a librarian for Oakland Public Library, in Oakland, CA. Visit Andrew at www.andrewdemcak.com

Made in the USA
Monee, IL
07 July 2026